HOW CELLS SEND, RECEIVE, AND PROCESS INFORMATION

MARC McLAUGHLIN,
MICHAEL FRIEDMAN,
AND BRETT FRIEDMAN

Britannica
Educational Publishing

Published in 2015 by Britannica Educational Publishing (a trademark of Encyclopædia Britannica, Inc.) in association with The Rosen Publishing Group, Inc.
29 East 21st Street, New York, NY 10010

Distributed exclusively by Rosen Publishing.
To see additional Britannica Educational Publishing titles, go to rosenpublishing.com.

First Edition

Britannica Educational Publishing
J.E. Luebering: Director, Core Reference Group
Anthony L. Green: Editor, Compton's by Britannica

Rosen Publishing
Hope Lourie Killcoyne: Executive Editor
Nelson Sá: Art Director
Brian Garvey: Designer
Cindy Reiman: Photography Manager
Karen Huang: Photo Researcher

Library of Congress Cataloging-in-Publication Data

McLaughlin, Marc, author.
How cells send, receive, and process information/Marc McLaughlin, Michael Friedman, and Brett Friedman.—First edition.
    pages cm.—(The Britannica guide to cell biology)
Includes bibliographical references and index.
ISBN 978-1-62275-800-5 (library bound)
1. Cytology—Juvenile literature. 2. Cell interaction—Juvenile literature. 3. Neurotransmitters—Juvenile literature. 4. Hormones—Juvenile literature. I. Friedman, Michael, 1955- author. II. Friedman, Brett, author. III. Title.
QH582.5.M315 2015
571.6—dc23

                                                                    2014021398

Cover (cell illustration) Mopic/Shutterstock.com; cover (background), pp. 1, 3, 4, 5 Sebastian Tomus/Shutterstock.com

Manufactured in the United States of America

CONTENTS

INTRODUCTION

Cells are the building blocks of the living world. Living things as different as bacteria, archaea, algae, fungi, protozoans, animals, and plants all consist of one or more cells. Cells are made up of parts that help living things to eat, respire, excrete wastes, and perform all the necessary functions of life. The parts are organized to fit and work together. For this reason, living things are called organisms.

The activities of the cells are controlled by the cell's genetic material—its deoxyribonucleic acid (DNA). DNA controls how the cell reproduces and functions and determines which traits are inherited from previous generations. In some types of organisms, called eukaryotes, the DNA is contained within a membrane-bound structure called the nucleus. In eukaryotic cells, most specialized tasks, such as obtaining energy from food molecules and producing material for cell growth, occur within a number of enclosed bodies called organelles. Plants, animals, fungi, and many microorganisms are eukaryotes.

Other microorganisms, namely bacteria and archaea, are unicellular (consisting of a single cell) and lack a distinct nucleus and organelles. These organisms are called prokaryotes. Some prokaryotic organisms, such as cyanobacteria (also called blue-green algae), can photosynthesize food; their food-making chlorophyll is scattered throughout the cell. In eukaryotic photosynthesizing organisms, such as plants and algae, the chlorophyll is contained within chloroplasts.

The parts of a multicellular organism are controlled so that they work together to keep the organism alive and aid in reproduction. In multicellular animals, such as humans, hormones regulate growth, keep muscles in condition, and perform many similar tasks. Other controls are carried out by nerve cells, also called

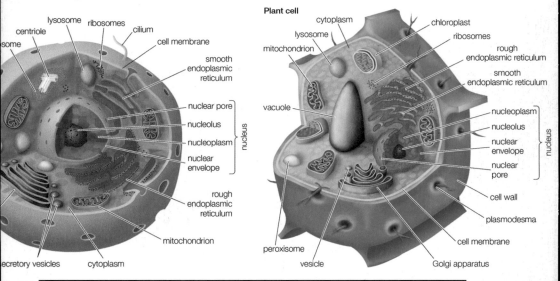

animal cell and plant cell

An animal cell (left) *and a plant cell contain an array of organelles. Some organelles and structures are specific to either cell, while others are found in both types.* Encyclopædia Britannica/Universal Images Group/Getty Images

neurons, via impulses to and from various parts of the body. These impulses can indicate that something has been seen, felt, or heard. They also make muscle cells contract or relax, so that animals can run, lie down, catch food, and do countless other things. Nerve cells may even deliver the impulses that stimulate hormone production. These specialized cells have most of the same features as other cells but have certain adaptations that help them do their respective jobs. Humans have many kinds of specialized cells, including red blood cells that transport oxygen throughout the body, skin cells that help to protect the body, muscle cells that contract and relax to move parts of the body, nerve cells that transport information from one part of the body to another, and pancreatic cells that produce compounds such as insulin. Specialized cells work with other similar cells to carry out their specific functions.

A cell functions similarly to the way in which a factory makes a product, with each factory worker performing a vital role. The most significant job performed in this so-called cell factory is the making of proteins. In eukaryotic cells, a variety of organelles, including the nucleus, ribosomes, Golgi apparatus, and endoplasmic reticulum, work together to manufacture proteins. These and other organelles enable the cell to send, receive, and process information so that it can maintain a stable equilibrium.

CHAPTER 1

THE MOLECULES DNA AND RNA

The cells of every living organism contain DNA, which determines how that organism will look and function. In humans, for instance, DNA tells the body what color an individual's eyes should be and how big that person's feet will grow, and it controls a variety of characteristics at a cellular level. Each different piece of information is carried on a specific segment of the DNA known as a gene, each of which contains biochemical codes for the synthesis of specific proteins.

DNA is a nucleic acid made up of two strands of biochemical units called nucleotides. Each nucleotide consists of a phosphate, deoxyribose (a sugar), and one of four nitrogen-bearing bases: adenine, guanine, cytosine, or thymine. Chemical bonds connect bases on one strand with bases on the other, forming base pairs. The molecule resembles a ladder with the two DNA strands for "sides" and chemical bonds forming "steps." The nucleotide ladder winds around itself, forming a double helix. This configuration makes the DNA molecule very stable.

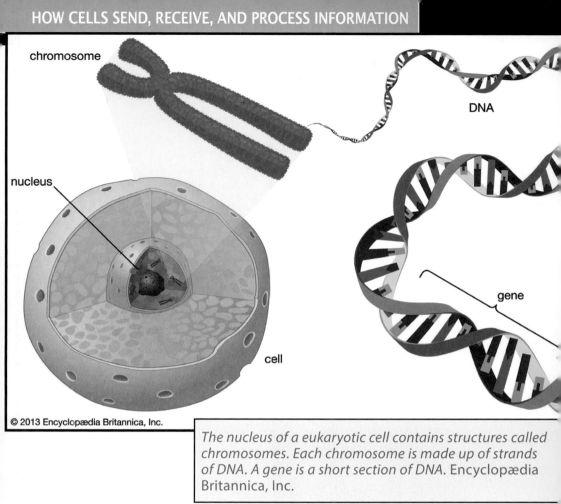

chromosome

DNA

nucleus

gene

cell

© 2013 Encyclopædia Britannica, Inc.

The nucleus of a eukaryotic cell contains structures called chromosomes. Each chromosome is made up of strands of DNA. A gene is a short section of DNA. Encyclopædia Britannica, Inc.

THE PRODUCTION OF DNA, THE GENETIC CODE, AND DNA'S WORK

When extra copies of DNA molecules are needed— as occurs before cell division—the molecule under- goes replication. In this process the two DNA strands separate—that is, the "rungs" of the ladder are broken.

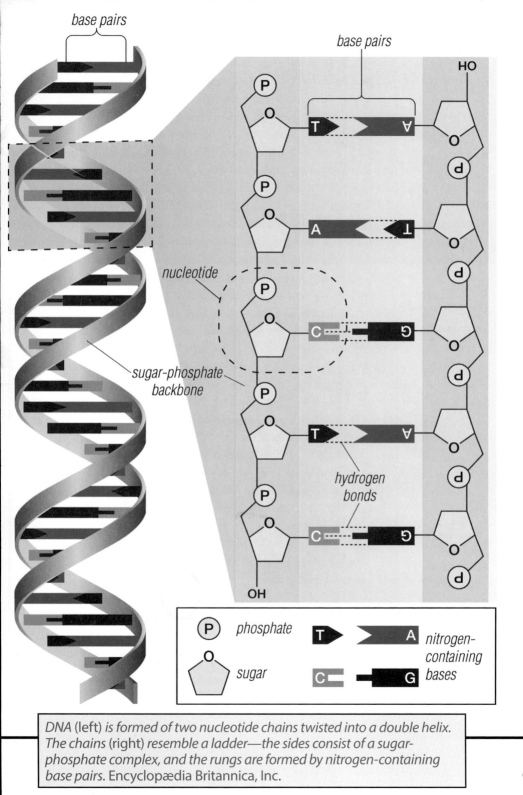

DNA (left) is formed of two nucleotide chains twisted into a double helix. The chains (right) resemble a ladder—the sides consist of a sugar-phosphate complex, and the rungs are formed by nitrogen-containing base pairs. Encyclopædia Britannica, Inc.

THE NUCLEUS

The nucleus is near the center of all eukaryotic cells. It is the control center of the cell and contains the DNA, which transmits hereditary traits. The nucleus usually has at least one nucleolus, a structure that is the site of RNA synthesis and storage.

The nucleus is enclosed by a two-layered membrane and contains a syrupy nucleoplasm. Its strands of DNA are wrapped around proteins in a manner that resembles a string of beads. Each strand contains a long series of genes—segments of DNA

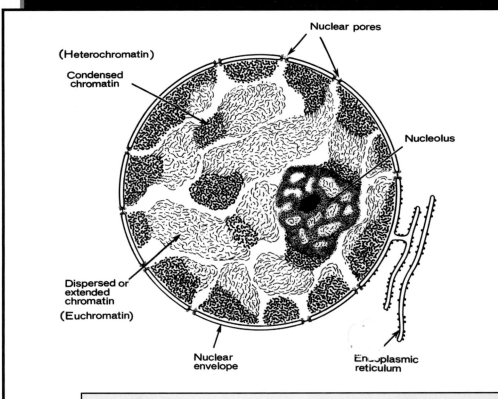

This diagram depicts the structural parts of an animal cell nucleus. The nucleus contains a nucleolus, surrounded by heterochromatin (chromosomal material that contains relatively few genes) and euchromatin (chromosomal material that contains the majority of active genes). The nuclear envelope encloses the nucleus and is pierced by nuclear pores. Don W Fawcett/Photo Researchers/ Getty Images

inherited from the previous generation. Genes determine the heritable characteristics of the organism. Genes also regulate cellular activities, including production of RNA, which in turn controls the manufacture of specific proteins.

The DNA strands, which are called chromatin because they readily stain with dyes, are usually too thin to be seen with an optical microscope. When a cell is ready to divide, the chromatin strands coil repeatedly around themselves and condense into thicker structures called chromosomes.

Each freed strand then serves as a template, or pattern, from which a new strand is produced. After the new strands are completed, each bonds to its respective template strand. This produces two new, identical DNA molecules, each consisting of one "old" strand and one new strand. This method of replication is a key factor in the stable transfer of genetic traits from one generation of cells to the next.

Genes contain instructions for making proteins, which are needed for growth, repair, and other functions. More specifically, the genes code for amino acids, the small molecules that form proteins.

Although more than 100 different amino acids exist in nature, only 20 are found in living organisms. This latter group is called the standard, or common, amino acids.

When the cell needs to make proteins, the DNA signals the appropriate gene to begin manufacturing ribonucleic acid (RNA). RNA is a single stranded molecule composed of the sugar component ribose instead of the deoxyribose found in DNA. Like DNA, it contains the bases guanine, cytosine, and adenine, though it has a base called uracil instead of thymine. To synthesize a protein, an RNA molecule called messenger RNA (mRNA) reads the appropriate DNA code in the gene. This code is then carried to an organelle known as a ribosome, where the mRNA serves as a template for the manufacture, or synthesis, of the new protein. During protein synthesis, two other forms of RNA work with mRNA—these are called transfer RNA (tRNA) and ribosomal RNA (rRNA).

CHAPTER 2

SOME CELL STRUCTURES AND THEIR ACTIVITIES

Cells contain cytoplasm, a substance made up of water, proteins, and other molecules surrounded by a membrane. In eukaryotic cells, the cytoplasm also contains many organelles, which perform most of the tasks necessary for keeping the cell alive.

CELLULAR MEMBRANES

A cell features several kinds of membranes. Its primary membrane, known as the cell (or plasma) membrane, encloses the entire cell and keeps it separate from its environment and from other cells. Other membranes encapsulate the organelles and can even be found inside certain organelles to increase their surface area.

Cellular membranes are made up mainly of two kinds of building blocks—proteins and lipids. Lipids are fatty-compound molecules that give the

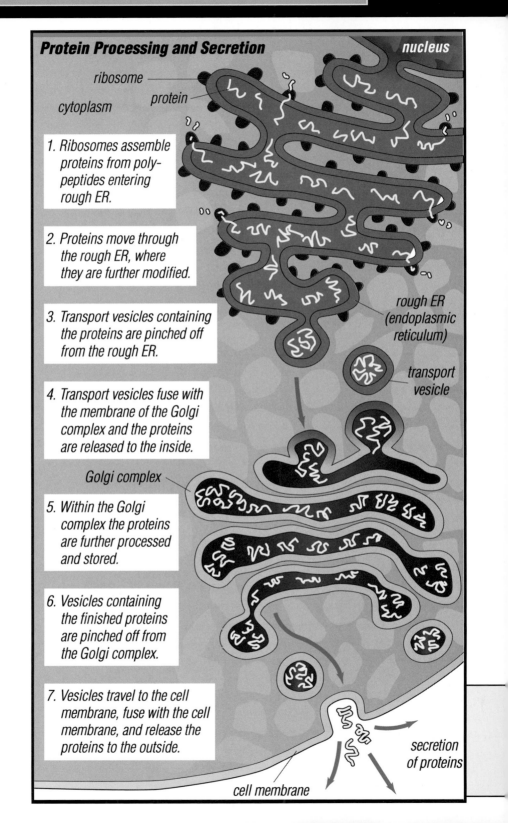

Protein Processing and Secretion

nucleus

ribosome

protein

cytoplasm

1. Ribosomes assemble proteins from polypeptides entering rough ER.

2. Proteins move through the rough ER, where they are further modified.

3. Transport vesicles containing the proteins are pinched off from the rough ER.

4. Transport vesicles fuse with the membrane of the Golgi complex and the proteins are released to the inside.

5. Within the Golgi complex the proteins are further processed and stored.

6. Vesicles containing the finished proteins are pinched off from the Golgi complex.

7. Vesicles travel to the cell membrane, fuse with the cell membrane, and release the proteins to the outside.

rough ER (endoplasmic reticulum)

transport vesicle

Golgi complex

secretion of proteins

cell membrane

membranes a double layer (known as the lipid bilayer) of protection and containment. Some of the proteins are structural and some transmit and receive signals from neighboring cells and the surrounding environment.

Most cellular membranes are semipermeable, meaning that while they keep most matter out, some materials are allowed in. Many of the membrane proteins form pores that function as gateways to allow or prevent the transport of substances across the membrane.

The membrane around the nucleus—also called the nuclear envelope—is also a double membrane (it has an outer and inner lipid bilayer). As with other membranes, the nuclear envelope makes it more difficult for most molecules to get in or out of the nucleus. It is dotted with pores through which only small proteins, ribosomal subunits, and RNA can pass. According to the British Society for Cell Biology, there are nearly 4,000 pores in a cell's nuclear envelope.

Although these pores are fully permeable to small molecules, they form a selective barrier against movement of larger molecules. Each pore is surrounded by an elaborate protein structure called the nuclear pore complex, which selects molecules for entrance into the nucleus. These complexes allow the nucleotide building blocks of DNA and RNA, as well as energy-carrying molecules for synthesizing genetic material, to enter the nucleus. Because the pores are not large enough for a complete ribosome to pass through, the ribosomal subunits must leave the nucleus separately

The endoplasmic reticulum (ER) plays a major role in the biosynthesis of proteins. Proteins that are synthesized by ribosomes on the ER are transported into the Golgi apparatus for processing. Some proteins will be secreted from the cell, others will be inserted into the plasma membrane, and still others will be inserted into lysosomes.
Encyclopædia Britannica, Inc.

PROTEINS

The precise number of protein types in the human body is unknown. However, scientists have isolated and described several thousands of them. Some are involved in the processes of growth, movement, reproduction, repair, digestion, and aging. Many proteins are enzymes—compounds that accelerate chemical reactions in and around cells. By following the instructions coded in genes, cells use their molecular machinery to build the proteins required by the organism. To do this, they need a supply of amino acids. Human adult cells can produce only 11 of their 20 necessary amino acids. The remaining nine—called essential amino acids—are obtained by eating foods that already contain them.

Some proteins, called transport proteins, carry substances throughout the cell and even from one place in the body to

Legumes, such as those in this bean salad, are a good source of essential amino acids. © Elenathewise/Fotolia

another. Hemoglobin, for example, is a transport protein in red blood cells that picks up oxygen as it circulates through lung tissue and then carries it to the body's cells. Other transport proteins are located in the cell membranes and shuttle nutrients and waste products from one side of the membrane to the other. Many proteins make up the supportive elements that provide biological structures with strength and protection.

and join together afterward. Some large proteins must also pass through the pores; these molecules have special amino acid sequences on their surface that signal admittance by the nuclear pore complexes.

RIBOSOMES

A ribosome is a structure whose parts are created in a specialized section of the nucleus called the nucleolus. Ribosomes are composed of two different sized subunits, each one comprising various proteins and rRNA. These subunits are assembled together outside the nucleus, forming a functional ribosome. Ribosomes manufacture protein and may float freely in the cytoplasm or may be incorporated into the membrane of an organelle known as the endoplasmic reticulum, which can aid in protein production.

THE ENDOPLASMIC RETICULUM

The endoplasmic reticulum (ER) is a large organelle that shares a membrane with the nucleus and resembles a series of flattened sacs inside the cytoplasm. The ER twists through the cytoplasm from the nuclear

Endoplasmic reticulum

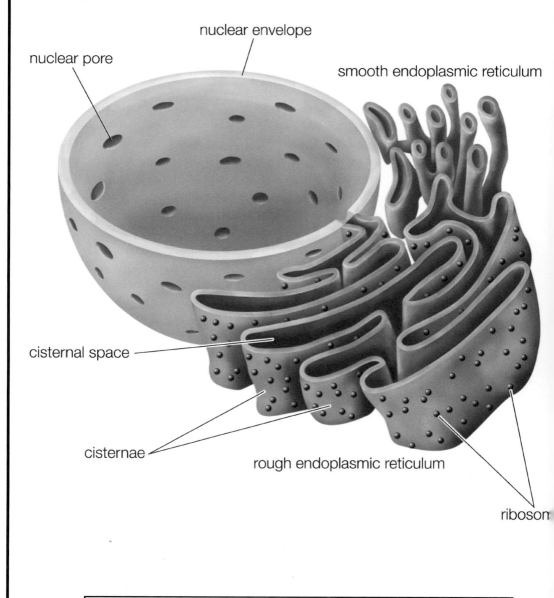

nuclear envelope

nuclear pore

smooth endoplasmic reticulum

cisternal space

cisternae

rough endoplasmic reticulum

riboson

A cutaway diagram shows the nuclear envelope and pores and the smooth and rough endoplasmic reticulum. Ribosomes on the outer surface of the endoplasmic reticulum play an essential role in protein synthesis within cells. Encyclopædia Britannica, Inc.

envelope to the cell membrane. The network serves as a highway for the movement of material within the cell and provides a convenient setting for the creation of proteins. The portion of the ER that helps in the synthesis of proteins is called the rough ER. It gets its name from the ribosomes that are attached to its surface. The portion of the ER that does not have ribosomes on its surface is called the smooth ER. It has an important function in cells that are involved in the synthesis and metabolism of lipids and the removal of the toxic substances of some drugs.

AMINO ACIDS AND PROTEIN SYNTHESIS

As described earlier, amino acids are the small molecules that form proteins. The eleven nonessential amino acids are synthesized in human cells during a process called transamination. This process involves the transferring of one amino acid group from one molecule to another. Amino acids float freely in a cell's cytoplasm and are brought to the ribosome by the transfer RNA (tRNA). Each tRNA molecule is designed to attract a particular amino acid, an ability that is determined by the nucleotides of the tRNA.

After the tRNA captures the amino acid, it guides it to a ribosome in the endoplasmic reticulum or to a free-floating ribosome in the cytoplasm. There, tRNA introduces the amino acid to the ribosome using a corresponding section of mRNA.

To create a working protein, another process, called translation, must take place in the ribosome. In translation, the ribosome, the tRNA, and the mRNA must work as a team to translate their encoded information

How DNA Directs Protein Synthesis

1. Double-Stranded DNA In the Cell Nucleus

2. Messenger RNA (mRNA) Forming on DNA Strands

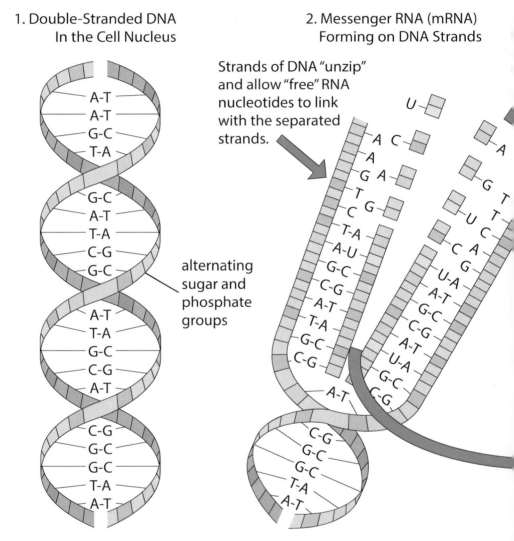

Strands of DNA "unzip" and allow "free" RNA nucleotides to link with the separated strands.

alternating sugar and phosphate groups

DNA and RNA constitute the genetic material of all living organisms. The steps for how DNA directs protein synthesis are illustrated here: 1) DNA in the cell nucleus carries a genetic code; 2) messenger RNA forms on DNA strands; 3) protein forms on the ribosomes. The synthesized protein finally is released to perform its task in the cell or elsewhere in the body.
Encyclopædia Britannica, Inc.

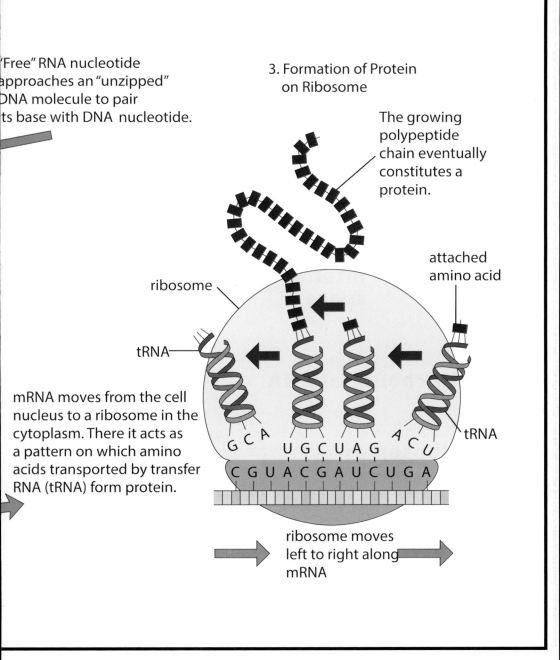

"Free" RNA nucleotide approaches an "unzipped" DNA molecule to pair its base with DNA nucleotide.

3. Formation of Protein on Ribosome

The growing polypeptide chain eventually constitutes a protein.

ribosome

attached amino acid

tRNA

mRNA moves from the cell nucleus to a ribosome in the cytoplasm. There it acts as a pattern on which amino acids transported by transfer RNA (tRNA) form protein.

tRNA

G C A   U G C U A G   A C U

C G U A C G A U C U G A

ribosome moves left to right along mRNA

MITOCHONDRION

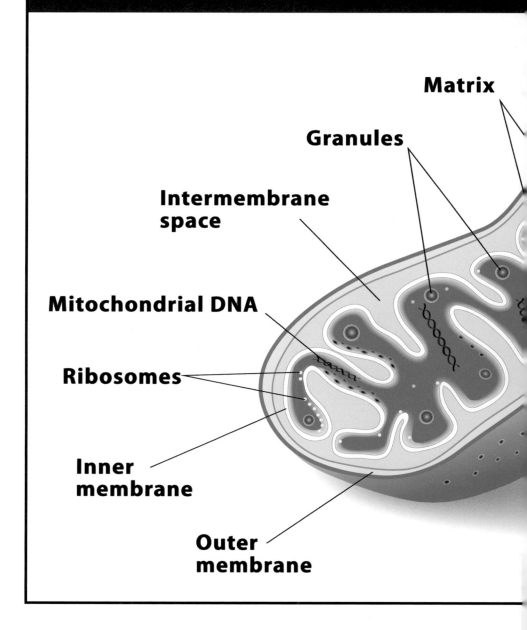

Matrix

Granules

Intermembrane space

Mitochondrial DNA

Ribosomes

Inner membrane

Outer membrane

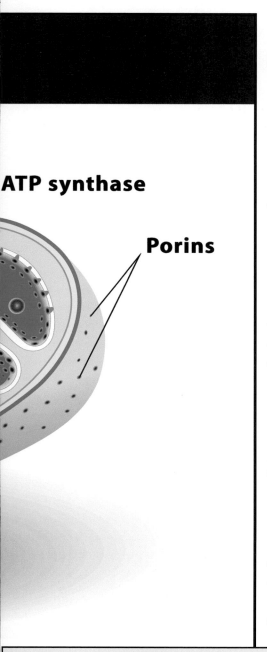

ATP synthase

Porins

into the specific protein requested by the DNA inside the nucleus.

The order of amino acids in a protein is what makes proteins different from each other. For example, a membrane protein has a different sequence of amino acids than a transport protein, and so on.

Ribosomes cannot work directly with amino acids to ensure that they are strung in the correct order. Instead, they match up the tRNA to the mRNA template. In this way, the message originally contained in the DNA becomes a reality.

SENDING PROTEINS TO THEIR FINAL DESTINATIONS

As soon as a portion of the amino acid sequence of a protein emerges from a ribosome, it is inspected for the

This cutaway diagram depicts the structures of a mitochondrion organelle that can be found in most eukaryotic cells. The mitochondria produce energy that the cell needs to function. They have an outer membrane and an inner membrane, which is folded. Designua/ Shutterstock.com

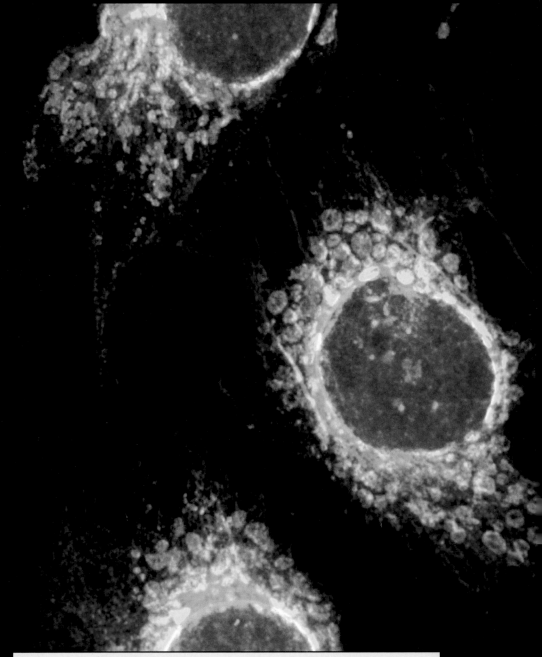

Microtubules, seen here in green, are hollow tubes inside cells. Microtubules play an important role in cytoplasmic streaming, or the movement of nutrients, proteins, and organelles within cells. Dr. Gopal Murti/Visuals Unlimited/Getty Images

presence of a signal known as a short endo-plasmic reticulum signal sequence. Proteins with this signal are immediately transferred to the interior of the ER, while those lacking the ER signal sequence are released from their ribosomes, directly into the cytoplasm.

The newly made proteins, whether in the cytoplasm or in the ER, are then sorted further according to additional signal sequences that they contain. Some of the proteins in the cytoplasm remain there, while others are transported into the sausage-shaped mito-chondria that produce the cell's energy. Further subsignals on these proteins then designate exactly where in the organelle the protein belongs. Proteins sorted into the ER have an even wider range of destinations. Some of them remain in the ER, where they function as part of the organelle, though most enter small sacs called transport vesi-cles and pass to the Golgi, the membranous organelle responsible for packaging proteins and other molecules for export from the cell. The Golgi retains some of the proteins for its unique functions, and the rest are packaged into vesicles and shipped to other destina-tions within the cell, such as the cell membrane.

CHAPTER 3

THE HORMONAL COMMUNICATION SYSTEM

Cells must "talk" with other cells to perform the functions necessary for survival. In multicellular organisms, the body's cells have established various methods of communicating. This communication between cells is called cell signaling. Cells have developed four different ways of communicating signals. These four methods are paracrine signaling, autocrine signaling, endocrine (hormonal) signaling, and synaptic (neuronal) signaling. In humans and other animals, the most common method is through the release of hormones.

CHEMICAL MESSENGERS

A hormone is a chemical created by a group of cells in one part of the body that encourages activity in another part of the body. In other words, it carries a message that tells a second group of cells to do something.

Not all cells release hormones, and those that do are found in structures called glands. When biologists

Signaling molecules (blue) travel between cells and allow them to respond to changes in their environment and coordinate a response. The four different signaling pathways are: at top left, cell communication over short distances (paracrine signaling); at upper right, communication between cells in physical contact or with cells that produced them (autocrine signaling); at bottom right, communication via nerve cells (synaptic signaling); and at bottom left, communication over long distances, via the bloodstream (endocrine signaling). Gunilla Elam/ Science Source

speak of all the glands in the body, they refer to them as the endocrine system. Glands release hormones only under certain circumstances. They may be prompted to release a hormone as a reaction to something that is taking place outside the body or in response to an internal event.

For the hormone to reach its target, it needs to travel in a bodily fluid such as the blood. Sometimes the hormone's target is very close to the gland where it is produced. In other instances, it may be very far away.

Once the hormone message enters the bloodstream, it is able to reach cells in many different parts of the body. However, not every part is capable of responding to the hormone message and usually only one type of cell can respond in the desired manner. The body ensures the desired response will happen through the cells' surface receptors. A surface receptor is a structure on the outside of a cell that designates the cell as the target for a particular hormone message. When the hormone reaches that target cell, it recognizes the receptor and delivers its information.

RECEPTORS AND SECOND MESSENGERS

Most hormones are released in small amounts and act slowly on their target cells. However, hormones do not actually enter a cell to achieve this change as they are too large to pass through the cell's outer membrane. How, then, can they get their message to the necessary organelle in the target cell? Hormones depend on the cell's surface receptors to pass the message along.

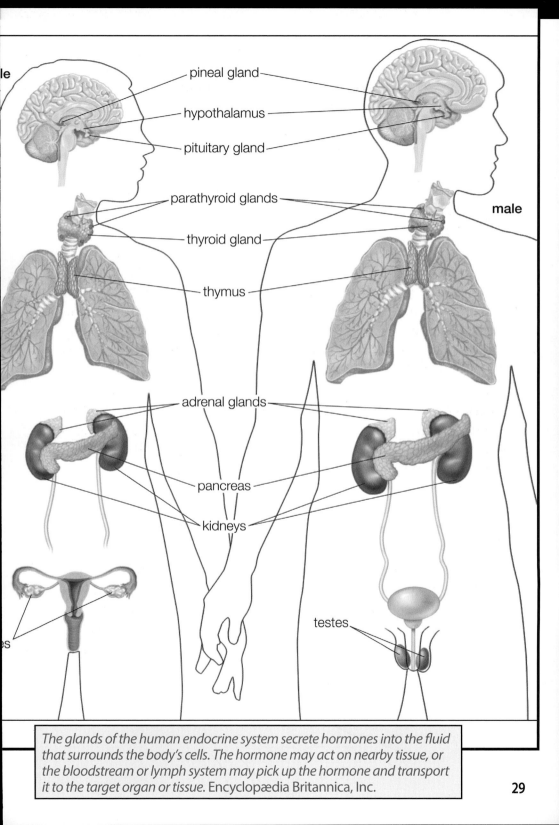

pineal gland

hypothalamus

pituitary gland

parathyroid glands

thyroid gland

thymus

adrenal glands

pancreas

kidneys

testes

male

The glands of the human endocrine system secrete hormones into the fluid that surrounds the body's cells. The hormone may act on nearby tissue, or the bloodstream or lymph system may pick up the hormone and transport it to the target organ or tissue. Encyclopædia Britannica, Inc.

29

ENDOCRINE GLANDS

The activities of the endocrine glands form one of the most complex systems in the human body. Although each gland has its own unique function, the glands of the endocrine system are interdependent and depend on the activity of the others. The hypothalamus produces several hormones, including those that regulate pituitary activity. The pituitary gland produces its own hormones that regulate growth and stimulate other endocrine glands. The adrenal glands, thyroid gland, testes, and ovaries are dependent upon pituitary stimulation. The hormones these glands produce govern metabolism, blood pressure, water and mineral balance, and reproductive functions, and they help defend against injury.

The term "hormone" comes from a Greek word meaning "to stir up." Hormones act as chemical messengers in creating a communication chain that links the body systems together, thus controlling and integrating the functions of the body.

Surface receptors are proteins that extend all the way through the cell membrane into the cell. Once a surface receptor receives a hormone message, it passes the message through the lipid bilayer into the cell, where another kind of message-carrying protein takes over. This molecule is called a second messenger and is designed to take the message from the surface receptor to its final destination inside the cell. Only after the message is delivered inside the cell can the target cell do the job that is required of it.

RECEIVING THE INCORRECT MESSAGE

Sometimes a target cell receives a hormone message when it shouldn't, causing it to work when it should be at rest. This miscommunication creates health problems for the human body.

One example of this occurrence is the hormonal disorder called acromegaly. Acromegaly typically affects middle-aged adults. It gets its name from the Greek words *acro*, or "extremities," and *megaly*, or "enlargement." One of its most common symptoms is the abnormal growth of the bones in the hands, feet, and head.

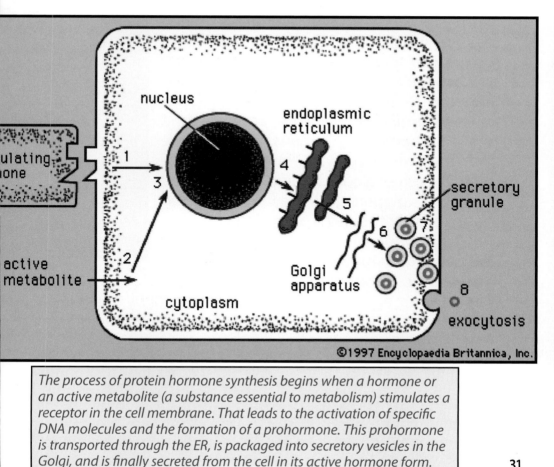

©1997 Encyclopaedia Britannica, Inc.

The process of protein hormone synthesis begins when a hormone or an active metabolite (a substance essential to metabolism) stimulates a receptor in the cell membrane. That leads to the activation of specific DNA molecules and the formation of a prohormone. This prohormone is transported through the ER, is packaged into secretory vesicles in the Golgi, and is finally secreted from the cell in its active hormone form. Encyclopædia Britannica, Inc.

31

Under normal circumstances, a person grows only during childhood and adolescence. A hormone known as IGF-1 causes an increase in cell size and cell number of most tissues, including bone, which continues until the child reaches adulthood. At that point, IGF-1 normally signals the pituitary gland to cut off production of growth hormone (GH). Sometimes, however, the pituitary gland continues to make GH. It is this continued production of GH by the overactive pituitary gland that results in abnormal growth, or in this case, acromegaly.

The first sign that someone is afflicted with acromegaly is usually a change in ring or shoe size. As the disease worsens, facial bones are affected. The brow and lower jaw start to stick out, the nose gets bigger, and the teeth grow farther apart. Other symptoms are weakness, headaches, and the enlargement of organs such as the liver, kidneys, and heart. People with acromegaly may also develop high blood pressure, diabetes, kidney stones, and arthritis and other joint problems.

The majority of acromegaly conditions are caused by tumors that are on the pituitary gland. Depending on the individual's case, treatment can include tumor removal by surgery and drug and radiation therapy. While some of the disease's effects may be reversed, others, unfortunately, are permanent.

In people with acromegaly, excessive GH is released long after the growth and development of a person's skeleton and organs are complete. Among the most noticeable signs of acromegaly are that the hands and feet get bigger. The woman whose feet are shown here has a tumor pressing on her pituitary gland that causes too much GH to be released.
Barcroft Media/Getty Images

CELL-TO-CELL COMMUNICATION BY CHEMICAL SIGNALING

Although hormones play an important role in cell-to-cell communication and enable cells to give instructions to a distant part of the body, they tend to act slowly over time. Cells close to each other sometimes need other, faster ways to send information.

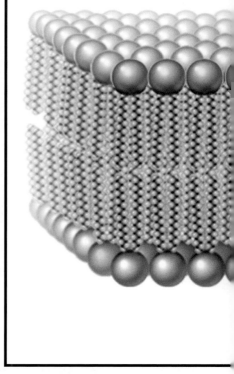

lipid bilayer

When similar cells are touching one another membrane-to-membrane, as is the case for many muscle or bone cells, they can communicate through small molecules (such as second messengers) sent back and forth. These molecules are admitted through the gap junctions in each cell's membrane.

Even when cells are not touching, they can send out small molecule messages to neighboring cells. The protein receptors on the receiving cells will then bind the molecular messages and take them in. These messages are known as paracrine signals (the prefix "para" means "beside" or "near"). Paracrine signals are used when cells in a particular part of the body need to act in a coordinated way. An example of paracrine signals is the chemical

phospholipid
molecule

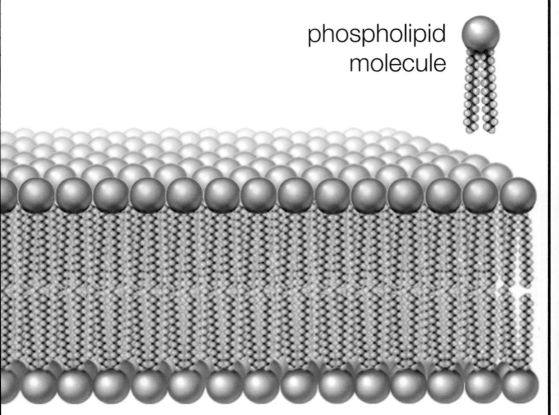

The cell membrane is composed of two thin layers of phospholipid molecules studded with large proteins. Phospholipids are chemically related to fats and oils. Some of the membrane proteins are structural; others form pores that function as gateways to allow or prevent the transport of substances across the membrane. Encyclopædia Britannica, Inc.

sent from nerve to muscle that causes the muscle to contract. In this instance, the muscle cells have regions specialized to receive the chemical signals from adjacent nerve cells.

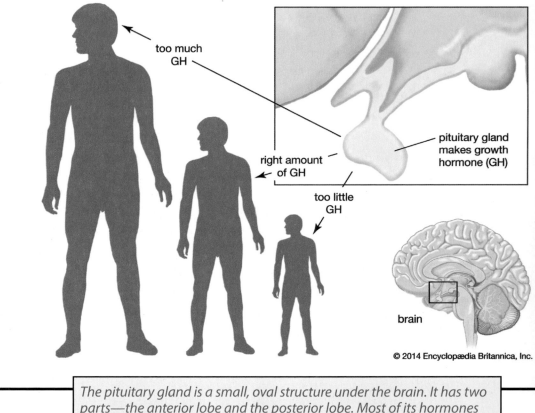

too much
GH

right amount
of GH

too little
GH

pituitary gland
makes growth
hormone (GH)

brain

© 2014 Encyclopædia Britannica, Inc.

The pituitary gland is a small, oval structure under the brain. It has two parts—the anterior lobe and the posterior lobe. Most of its hormones are made in its anterior lobe. Growth hormone (GH) is essential for normal physical growth in children. Encyclopædia Britannica, Inc.

In certain cases, a signal may act on the cell that produced it. When molecules act on the same cells that made them, they are called autocrine signals (the prefix "auto" means "self"). Autocrine signals include molecules outside the cell and various factors that encourage cell growth. In both autocrine and paracrine signaling, the chemical signal works in the immediate vicinity of the cell that produces it and is present at high concentrations.

Unicellular organisms, such as archaea, bacteria, protozoa, and some algae and fungi, adapt and respond to their environments. One of the ways they do this is through intercellular (between two or more cells) communication. This communication between two or more unicellular organisms allows them to respond appropriately to signals in their environment and coordinate their activities. The communication is achieved through the secretion (release) of extracellular signals known as pheromones—chemicals that trigger a social response in members of the same species. Like multicellular organisms, unicellular organisms must maintain homeostasis. This is the maintaining of stable and constant internal conditions, such as temperature regulation and pH balancing (balancing of acidity and alkalinity) that allow the cell to function and perform the life processes necessary to survival— intake of nutrients, converting of nutrients to energy, excretion, reproduction, etc. Signaling in unicellular organisms enables populations of cells (or colonies) to coordinate with one another, share information about the surrounding environment, and thereby optimize the carrying out of the life processes and the chances for reproduction and species survival.

CHAPTER 4

NEURONS, NEUROTRANSMITTERS, AND SYNAPSES

Though paracrine signals act more quickly than hormonal (or endocrine) signals, some cells need an even faster system to carry out the tasks that are assigned to them.

These cells are called nerve cells, or neurons, and are found in the body's nervous system. The nervous system includes two main parts: the central nervous system, which consists of the brain and the spinal cord, and the peripheral nervous system, which are the nerves that relay impulses between the central nervous system and the rest of the body. Neurons use special kinds of amino acids called neurotransmitters to send nerve impulses, or electrical signals, from one neuron to another.

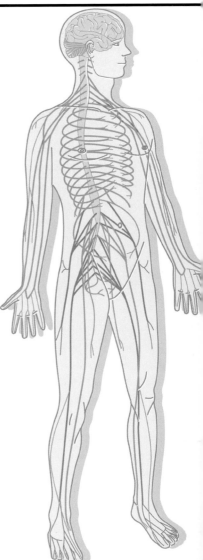

Signals transferred by neurotransmitters travel very rapidly. Sometimes they move more than 250 mph (402 kmh)—faster than a Formula One racing car! However, neurotransmitters work only over very short distances. In this way they are different from hormones, which may have to travel from one end of the body to the other.

Neurotransmitters are also different from hormones in that they can be released on a conscious basis. For instance, when a person makes an effort to remember something, neurotransmitters are sent from neuron to neuron in the brain. Hormones, on the other hand, are automatically released. People cannot send them out at will.

THE MAKEUP OF NEURONS

The average human brain is composed of nearly 86 billion neurons. These neurons are very small, although they do vary in shape and size. They usually have a round or pyramid-shaped cell body, which contains the nucleus and other basic cell parts. In many ways, neurons are similar to other cells in the body. For instance, they are surrounded by a cell membrane and they contain mitochondria, an endoplasmic reticulum, and other organelles. However, neurons also differ from other cells in the body.

Unlike other cells, neurons have special parts that stick out from the main body of the cell, similar to "trees" of branching fibers. These sprouts are called

The nervous system in humans is made up of the central nervous system (the brain and the spinal cord) and the peripheral nervous system, which comprises the cranial nerves (except for the optic nerves), the spinal nerves, and the autonomic nervous system, which controls actions that are mostly automatic, such as breathing and heart rate. BSIP/Universal Images Group/Getty Images

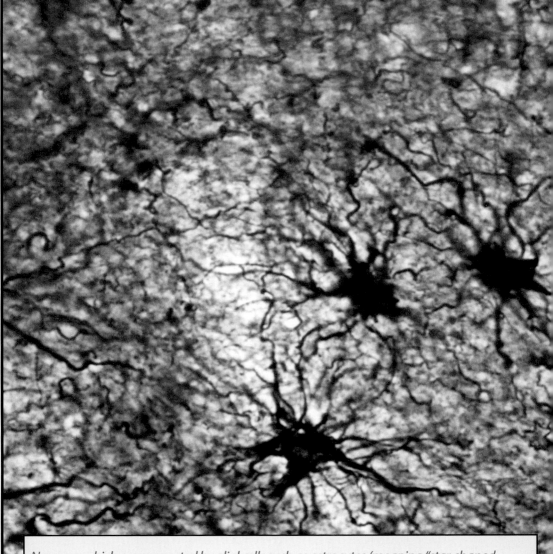

Neurons, which are supported by glial cells such as astrocytes (meaning "star-shaped cells"), retain the ability to deviate from the usual functions and to reorganize themselves in response to new information. Biophoto Associates/Photo Researchers/Getty Images

dendrites. Dendrites have a rough surface and receive nerve impulses of information and conduct them toward the cell body. Besides the dendrites, long tube-like fibers called axons extend from the cell body. Axons have a smooth surface and carry the nerve

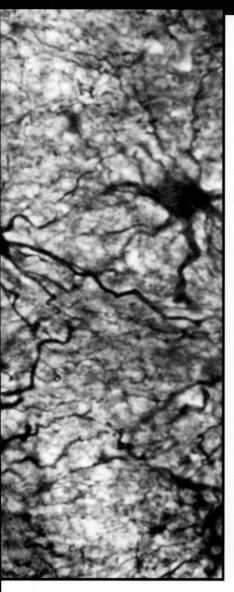

impulses of information away from the cell bodies to other cells. Generally, a neuron will have only one axon but many dendrites.

SYNAPSES

To communicate with one another, neurons form a special connection at a junction called a synapse. The synapse is the gap the neurotransmitter must cross when it carries information from neuron to neuron. Every synapse consists of three parts.

The first part of the synapse is called the presynaptic membrane of the axon of one neuron. This is the part of the neuron that sends messages and contains neurotransmitters.

The second part of the synapse is the postsynaptic membrane. This part is on the dendrite of the receiving neuron, which contains special receptors. These receptors act as targets for the neurotransmitters.

The third part of the synapse is the synaptic cleft, which is the tiny gap between the presynaptic membrane and the postsynaptic membrane. It is this space that the neurotransmitter must cross to reach the receiving neuron.

NEURONS AND NEUROGENESIS

For years it was thought that the brain was a closed, fixed system. Only a handful of discoveries, primarily in rats, birds, and primates, in the latter half of the twentieth century hinted at

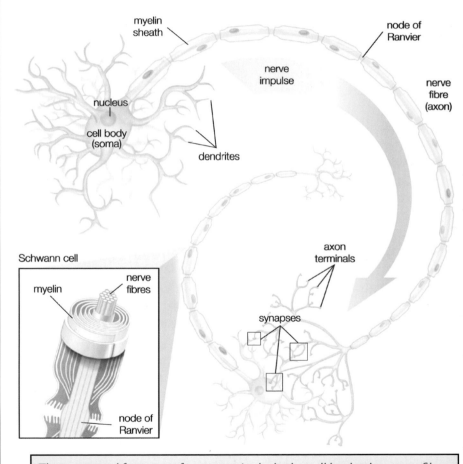

The structural features of a neuron include the cell body, the nerve fiber, or axon, and the dendrites. A Schwann cell is any of the cells in the peripheral nervous system that produce the myelin sheath around neuronal axons. The node of Ranvier is the periodic gap in the myelin sheath. Encyclopædia Britannica, Inc.

the regenerative, or regrowth, capability of brain cells. Scientists assumed that once the brain was damaged or impaired, it could not regenerate new cells. Though other types of cells, such as liver and skin cells, are able to regenerate, it was thought that adult brain cells could not regenerate as it would be impossible for a new cell to fully integrate itself into the existing complex system. It was not until 1998 that neural stem cells (NSCs) were discovered in humans. NSCs have the potential to give rise to offspring cells that grow and differentiate into neurons and glial cells. They were found first in a region of the brain called the hippocampus, which was known to be instrumental in forming memories. NSCs were

(continued on the next page)

A fluorescence microscope with a digital camera was used to photograph neural stem cells in a culture dish. The cells are migrating out of a cluster of neural stem cells, called a neurosphere. This type of cell is being studied for use in cell therapy for traumatic brain injuries and Parkinson's disease. Riccardo Cassiani-Ingoni/ Science Photo Library Getty Images

(continued from the previous page)

later also found to be active in the olfactory bulbs (an area that processes smell) and inactive in the septum (an area that processes emotion), the striatum (an area that processes movement), and the spinal cord.

Clinically effective treatments that can directly repair the damaged brain in people who have traumatic brain injury are lacking. Stem cells or genetically modified cells (for example, glial cells) could be transplanted into the zone of injury in an attempt to replace damaged cells with substitute neurons or other cells that can restore function.

However, neurotransmitters do not generally cross the synaptic cleft independently. They need a push in the form of an electrical impulse. This electrical impulse is generated within the message-sending neuron and travels down the axon to the presynaptic membrane. One impulse is enough to send a number of neurotransmitters shooting across the synaptic cleft.

As the neurotransmitters move into the space between the neurons, they spread out. This spreading enables them to reach more than one of the receptors located on the postsynaptic membrane. This action is important because it will take more than one neurotransmitter to get the desired response.

When a neurotransmitter reaches a receptor, it creates a change in the receiving neuron. It makes that neuron more likely to follow the directions contained in the neurotransmitter. If enough neurotransmitters reach the receiving neuron with the same message, it will

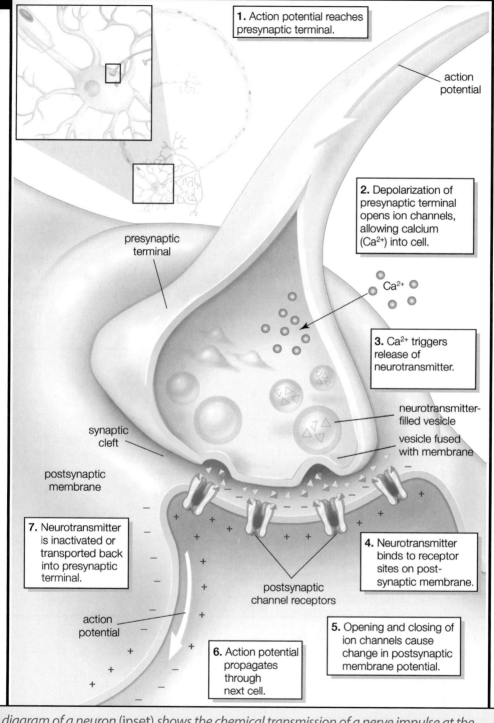

1. Action potential reaches presynaptic terminal.

action potential

2. Depolarization of presynaptic terminal opens ion channels, allowing calcium (Ca²⁺) into cell.

Ca²⁺

3. Ca²⁺ triggers release of neurotransmitter.

presynaptic terminal

neurotransmitter-filled vesicle

vesicle fused with membrane

synaptic cleft

postsynaptic membrane

7. Neurotransmitter is inactivated or transported back into presynaptic terminal.

4. Neurotransmitter binds to receptor sites on post-synaptic membrane.

postsynaptic channel receptors

action potential

5. Opening and closing of ion channels cause change in postsynaptic membrane potential.

6. Action potential propagates through next cell.

A diagram of a neuron (inset) *shows the chemical transmission of a nerve impulse at the synapse. The arrival of the nerve impulse at the presynaptic terminal stimulates the release of a neurotransmitter into the synaptic gap. The binding of the neurotransmitter to the receptors on the postsynaptic membrane stimulates the regeneration of the action potential in the postsynaptic neuron.* Encyclopædia Britannica, Inc.

45

Nerve Impulses Pass from Neuron to Neuron at the Synapses

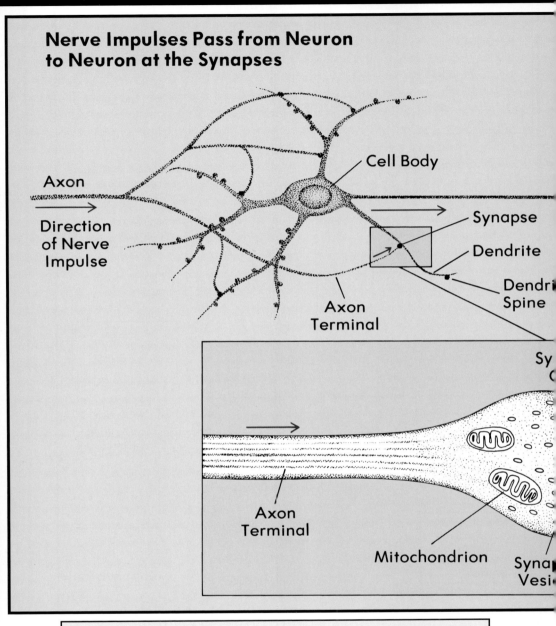

Axon

Direction
of Nerve
Impulse

Cell Body

Synapse

Dendrite

Dendri
Spine

Axon
Terminal

Sy

Axon
Terminal

Mitochondrion

Syna
Vesi

This close-up view shows a synapse and its parts between two neurons. An impulse reaching the axon terminal of a neuron triggers a chemical release from the synaptic vesicles, and the chemical then bridges the synaptic cleft and causes electrical changes that may start or prevent an impulse in the next neuron. Encyclopædia Britannica, Inc.

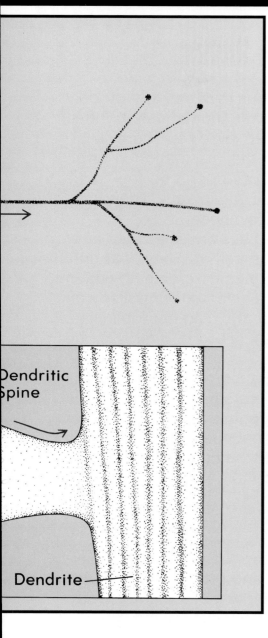

Dendritic
Spine

Dendrite

create what scientists call an action potential, and the neuron will send out an electrical impulse of its own. In this way, it passes on the message contained in the neurotransmitters. Action potentials travel faster in some neurons than in others. The transmission speeds range from about 3 to 330 ft (1 to 100 m) per second—or about 2 to 225 mph (3 to 360 kph). The speed varies depending on the properties of the nerve fiber and its environment. In general, nerve impulses travel faster along thicker nerve fibers. Many axons are covered with an insulating membrane called the myelin sheath. The myelin sheath covers sections of the axon, which are separated by short segments of bare axon called nodes. In an axon with a myelin sheath, the action potential jumps from one node to the next instead of traveling along the entire length of the axon. This jumping increases the speed at which the impulse can travel.

PRECISION IS CRUCIAL

Communication in the nervous system is not only faster than other kinds of cellular communication within the body but also much more precise. There is no chance of the neuron getting the information in error. This is because neurons do not depend on the "public" bloodstream to carry their messages. They have their own private channel: the synapse.

In addition, neurons do not pass on a message after they receive a single neurotransmitter. They wait until they have received enough of them to create an action potential. Then they send out an electrical impulse that allows the message to move to the next neuron in line. This communication between neurons needs to be controlled and efficient because the ability to make quick decisions is necessary for a body's survival. Some research scientists estimate that each neuron in the brain has up to 10,000 connections to another brain cell. These scientists continue to study neuron connections to try to decipher the code of the brain.

THE ORDERLY FUNCTIONS OF A COMPLEX NETWORK

Effective cells send, receive, and process information to contribute to the smooth working of the entire body. From DNA codes that are responsible for the production of proteins to the various messages that pass from cell to cell, inter- and intracellular communication is essential for the survival of individual cells and the

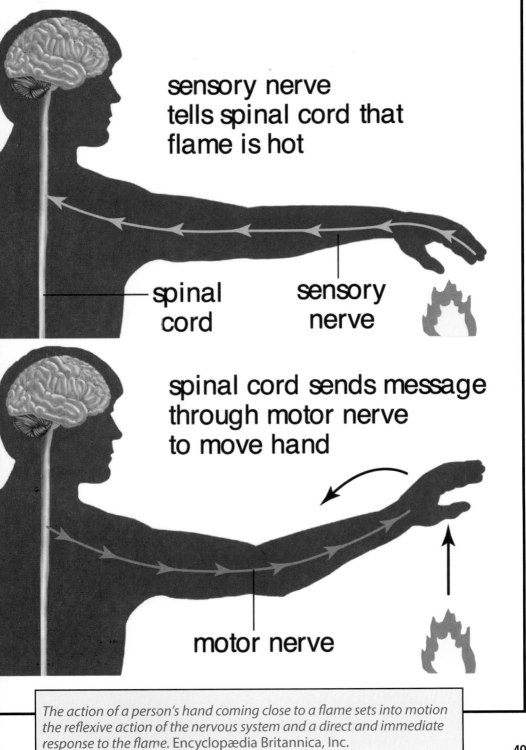

sensory nerve
tells spinal cord that
flame is hot

spinal
cord

sensory
nerve

spinal cord sends message
through motor nerve
to move hand

motor nerve

The action of a person's hand coming close to a flame sets into motion the reflexive action of the nervous system and a direct and immediate response to the flame. Encyclopædia Britannica, Inc.

49

organisms they comprise. When any of these message systems is prevented from doing its job, the entire body suffers. In some cases, these failures may even lead to death.

When hormones and neurotransmitters pass information along smoothly and efficiently, the body works like a well-rehearsed orchestra. When one instrument plays off-key, the rest of the orchestra sounds out of tune. All the instruments contribute to the sound of the orchestra so it is balanced. The body's systems and organs are interconnected, too, and if one organ does not work as it should, it affects the balance of the rest of the body. This comparison is true for the body's cells, which must carry messages from one cell to another so that information goes where it needs to seamlessly.

GLOSSARY

amino acid Any one of many acids that occur naturally in living things and that include some that form proteins.

base Any of various compounds that react with an acid to form a salt, have a bitter taste, and turn litmus paper blue.

bond A means by which atoms, ions, or groups of atoms are held together in a molecule or crystal.

chromosome One of the rod-shaped or threadlike DNA-containing bodies of a cell nucleus that contains all or most of the genes of an organism and can be seen especially during cell division.

cytosol The fluid portion of the cytoplasm exclusive of organelles and membranes.

double helix The arrangement in space of DNA that resembles a spirally twisted ladder with the sides made up of the sugar and phosphate units of the two nucleotide strands and the rungs made up of the pyrimidine and purine bases extending into the center and joined by hydrogen bonds.

equilibrium A state in which opposing forces or actions are balanced so that one is not stronger or greater than the other.

essential amino acid An amino acid that is necessary for proper growth of the animal body and that cannot be made by the body in sufficient amounts but must be obtained from food containing proteins.

evolve To change or develop slowly, often into a better, more complex, or more advanced state.

gene A part of DNA or sometimes RNA that is usually located on a chromosome and that contains chemical information needed to make a particular protein (as an enzyme) controlling or influencing an inherited bodily trait or activity (as eye color or metabolism) or that influences or controls the activity of another gene or genes.

genetic code The chemical code that is the basis of genetic inheritance and consists of units of three linked chemical groups that specify particular kinds of amino acids used to make proteins or that start or stop the process of making proteins.

hormone A natural substance that is produced in the body and that influences the way the body grows or develops; an artificial substance that acts like a hormone.

lipid Any of various substances (as fats and waxes) that with proteins and carbohydrates make up the principal structural parts of living cells.

membrane A thin, soft, flexible sheet or layer especially of a plant or animal part (as a cell, tissue, or organ).

metabolism The chemical processes by which a plant or an animal uses food, water, etc., to grow and heal and to make energy.

mitochondrion (plural, **mitochondria**) One of the round or long bodies found in the cytoplasm of cells outside the nucleus that are rich in fats, proteins, and enzymes and are important centers of metabolic processes that use oxygen and produce energy.

molecule The smallest particle of a substance having all the characteristics of the substance.

neurogenesis The development of nerves, nervous tissue, or the nervous system.

nucleotide Any of the basic units of structure of DNA or RNA that consist of a base (as adenine, cytosine, guanine, or thymine) joined to a sugar (as deoxyribose) with five carbon atoms in a molecule and to a phosphate group.

nucleus The central part of most cells that contains genetic material and is enclosed in a membrane.

organelle A structure (as a mitochondrion) in a cell that performs a special function.

permeable Having pores or openings that permit liquids or gases to pass through.

photosynthesize To synthesize, or make by combining, chemical compounds with the aid of radiant energy and especially light.

replication An act or process of copying or duplication.

respire To breathe, or to take up oxygen and produce carbon dioxide through oxidation.

ribonucleic acid (RNA) Any of various nucleic acids that are typically found in the cytoplasm of cells, are usually composed of a single chain of nucleotides, differ from DNA in containing ribose as the five-carbon sugar instead of deoxyribose, and function mostly in protein synthesis.

ribosome One of numerous small RNA-containing particles in a cell that are sites of protein synthesis.

synthesize To make something from simpler substances through a chemical process.

template A gauge, pattern, or mold (as a thin plate or board) used as a guide to form a piece being made.

transamination In this process, the DNA normally involved in hereditary processes directs the placement of amino acids in a specific sequence to form a molecule of protein.

transcription The process of forming a messenger RNA molecule using a DNA molecule as a guide.

translation The process of forming a protein molecule from information contained in a messenger RNA molecule.

FOR MORE INFORMATION

American Association for the Advancement of Science (AAAS)
1200 New York Avenue NW
Washington, DC 20005
(202) 326-6400
Website: http://www.aaas.org
The AAAS promotes science and technology around the world. It sponsors a K–12 STEM educational resource called Science NetLinks, which offers lesson plans for teachers, videos for students, interactive activities, and podcasts on science-related subjects.

American Institute of Biological Sciences (AIBS)
1900 Campus Commons Drive, Suite 200
Reston, VA 20191
(703) 674-2500
Website: http://www.aibs.org
The AIBS encourages biological research and education for everyone's well-being. It supports educational programs in biology, and its website provides online articles on a variety of genetics topics and ethics.

The American Society for Cell Biology (ASCB)
8120 Woodmont Avenue, Suite 750
Bethesda, MD 20814-2762
(301) 347-9310
Website: http://www.ascb.org
The ASCB helps to advance scientific studies and promotes good research policies worldwide. Its website

includes an interactive image library of cells, their structures, and their functions.

Brain Canada
2155 Guy Street, Suite 900
Montreal, QC H3H 2R9
Canada
(514) 989-2989
Website: http://braincanada.ca
Brain Canada promotes institutional and public research in the neurosciences. On its website, it provides fact sheets about the human brain and neuroscience.

Canadian Society for Molecular Biosciences (CBS)
c/o Rofail Conference and Management Services
17 Dossetter Way
Ottawa, ON K1G 4S3
Canada
(613) 421-7229
Website: http://www.csmb-scbm.ca
The CBS encourages the study of biochemistry. It offers financial support to graduate student organizations involved in cell biology, genetics, molecular biology, and biochemistry. It also sponsors student research conferences, career fairs, and scientific symposium days.

Genetics Society of America
9650 Rockville Pike
Bethesda, MD 20814-3998
(301) 634-7079

Website: http://www.genetics-gsa.org
This organization for researchers and educators in the
field of genetics offers educational and outreach
materials and promotes research in colleges, gov-
ernmental organizations, and private research
institutions. It publishes the journals *GENETICS* and
G3: Genes/Genomes/Genetics.

National Institutes of Health (NIH)
9000 Rockville Pike
Bethesda, MD 20892
(301) 496-4000
Website: http://www.nih.gov
The NIH is a division of the U.S. Department of Health
and Human Services. It encourages research to
improve the public's health and provides health
information and educational resources on its website, including material about blood cells and
disorders.

The Protein Society
1450 South Rolling Road, Suite 3.007
Baltimore, MD 21227
(443) 543-5450
Website: http://www.proteinsociety.org
This not-for-profit organization encourages scholarly
cooperation among scientists who examine and
study proteins. Its website provides resources for
students who are interested in studying proteins,
including the Proteopedia, a free 3-D encyclopedia
of proteins and other molecules.

Society for Neuroscience
1121 14th Street NW, Suite 1010
Washington, DC 20005
(202) 962-4000
Website: http://www.sfn.org
This society of scientists and doctors is focused on
    studying the brain and nervous system. It supports
    educational programs that award high school stu-
    dents' accomplishments in brain science learning.

WEBSITES

Because of the changing nature of Internet links, Rosen
Publishing has developed an online list of websites
related to the subject of this book. This site is updated
regularly. Please use this link to access this list:

http://www.rosenlinks.com/BGCB/Send

FOR FURTHER READING

Allen, Terence, and Graham Cowling. *The Cell: A Very Short Introduction.* New York, NY: Oxford University Press, 2011.

Ballard, Carol. *Cells and Cell Function.* New York, NY: Rosen Publishing, 2010.

Ballen, Karen Gunnison. *Decoding Our DNA: Craig Venter vs. the Human Genome Project* (Scientific Rivalries and Scandals). Minneapolis, MN: Twenty-First Century Books, 2013.

CK–12 Foundation. *Human Biology—Lives of Cells.* Kindle Edition. Palo Alto, CA: CK–12 Foundation, 2012.

Claybourne, Anna. *The Usborne Complete Book of the Human Body.* London, England: Usborne Publishing, Ltd., 2013.

Cobb, Allan B. *Cell Theory* (Science Foundations). New York, NY: Chelsea House Publishers, 2011.

Gerdes, Louise. *Human Genetics* (Opposing Viewpoints). Farmington Hills, MI: Greenhaven Press, 2014.

Guttman, Burton, Anthony Griffiths, David Suzuki, and Tara Cullis. *Genetics: The Code of Life* (Contemporary Issues). New York, NY: Rosen Publishing, 2011.

Inge, Bill. *A–Z Biology Handbook.* 4th ed. Digital Ed. Abingdon, England: Bookpoint Ltd., 2014.

Mooney, Carla. *Genetics: Breaking the Code of Your DNA* (Inquire and Investigate). White River Junction, VT: Nomad Press, 2014.

Moore, Pete. *Stem Cell Research* (Ethical Debates). New York, NY: Rosen Publishing, 2012.

Nelson, Maria. *Cells Up Close*. Buffalo, NY: Gareth Stevens, 2014.

Newman, Michael E. *Cells and Human Health* (Cells: The Building Blocks of Life). New York, NY: Chelsea House Publishers, 2012.

Panno, Joseph. *The Cell: Nature's First Life-Form* (New Biology). Rev. ed. New York, NY: Facts On File, 2010.

Rogers, Kara, ed. *The Brain and the Nervous System* (The Human Body). New York, NY: Britannica Educational Publishing and Rosen Educational Services, 2011.

Rogers, Kara, ed. *The Cell* (Introduction to Biology). New York, NY: Britannica Educational Publishing and Rosen Educational Services, 2011.

Rogers, Kara, ed. *The Endocrine System* (The Human Body). New York, NY: Britannica Educational Publishing and Rosen Educational Services, 2012.

Silverstein, Alvin, Virginia Silverstein, and Laura Silverstein Nunn. *Cells* (Science Concepts). Minneapolis, MN: Twenty-First Century Books, 2009.

Snedden, Robert. *Understanding the Brain and the Nervous System* (Understanding the Human Body). New York, NY: Rosen Publishing, 2010.

Stimola, Aubrey. *Brain Injuries* (Understanding Brain Diseases and Disorders). New York, NY: Rosen Publishing, 2012.

Stimola, Aubrey. *Cell Biology.* New York, NY : Rosen Publishing, 2011.

Time Editors. *The Science of You: The Factors that Shape Your Personality.* New York, NY: Time Books, 2013.

Wanjie, Anne, ed. *The Basics of Cell Biology* (Core Concepts). New York, NY: Rosen Publishing, 2014.

Watkins, Christine. *Addiction* (Opposing Viewpoints). Farmington Hills, MI: Greenhaven Press, 2014.

Wilson, Michael R. *The Endocrine System: Hormones, Growth, and Development* (The Library of Sexual Health). New York, NY: Rosen Publishing, 2009.

Wilson, Michael R. *Frequently Asked Questions About How the Teen Brain Works* (Teen Life). New York, NY: Rosen Publishing, 2010.

INDEX